Old TUXFORD and LAX

by
David Ottewell

This photograph of the market place was either taken early in the morning or on a Sunday, as the roads are empty and the Excelda Cafe is shut.

First published in the United Kingdom, 2004,
by Stenlake Publishing Ltd.
Telephone: 01290 551122
Printed by Cordfall Ltd., Glasgow, G21 2QA

ISBN 1 84033 325 1

FURTHER READING

The books listed below were used by the author during his research. None of them are available from Stenlake Publishing. Those interested in finding out more are advised to contact their local bookshop or reference library.

Beckett, J. V., *A History of Laxton*, Basil Blackwell, 1989
Bird, J., *Studies in the Evolution of Tuxford*, Eaton Hall College of Education, 1968
Keeton, A. W., *Laxton and its Past*
Orwin, C. S. & C. S., *The History of Laxton*, Oxford University Press, 1935
Swift., Revd Canon T. W., *Some of Our Yesterdays: The Story of Tuxford and its Church*
Trustees of the Laxton Visitors Centre, *Laxton*, 1979

Tuxford's churchyard was extended by half an acre in 1903, and this was the site chosen when the town erected a memorial to commemorate local men who lost their lives in the First World War. The unveiling took place in 1920.

INTRODUCTION

Tuxford, situated twenty-eight miles north-north-east of Nottingham, has had an interesting history having been both a market town and a post town.

In the early twentieth century arrowheads and flints were unearthed, and Roman coins have been found locally suggesting a Romano–British site in the vicinity. By the time of the Domesday Book (1086) the settlement was known as Tuxfarne. The quality of the local soil led to many people calling the town Tuxford in the Clay.

The Manor of Tuxford had been acquired by the de Lexington family by the twelfth century. It was already an important centre by this time, and in 1218 Henry III granted it rights to hold one of the earliest charter fairs. Later two famous Nottinghamshire families, the Markhams and the Suttons, became lords of the manor of Tuxford. By the reign of Henry VIII control had passed to the White family via the female line of the Suttons.

Tuxford's situation on the Great North Road meant that it was a stopping off point for many important travellers. In 1503 Princess Margaret, sister of Henry VIII, stayed in the town whilst travelling to Scotland. During the Civil War both Charles I and his wife visited Tuxford. In the nineteenth century local MP William Gladstone used the town as the point to join the overnight coach to London, and the Prince of Wales, later Edward VII, passed through Tuxford on his way to stay at Rufford Abbey.

The 60 years from 1801 to 1861 saw the population of Tuxford rise from 785 to 1,304, based mainly on the prosperity generated from agriculture and catering for travellers. The first half of the nineteenth century saw the town's heyday as a staging post on the Great North Road, with eleven hotels and inns being listed in trade directories. In 1820 the Duke of Newcastle, based at Clumber Park, became lord of the manor.

The arrival of rail travel saw a notable dropping off in road usage, and by 1869 only six inns were still operating in Tuxford. However, the railways also brought considerable advantages. The town's central location meant that four different companies built stations in Tuxford, and a large proportion of the adult male workforce was employed by railway companies, although by 1891 the population had slipped to 938.

A hundred years after the decline in road travel, rail cutbacks and closures meant that many railway workers were made redundant. Fortunately the 1960s saw nearby Bevercotes colliery begin full production and High Marnham power station start operations. In the event so many new jobs were created that additional workers were attracted to Tuxford, new housing was built, and by 1988 the population of the town was estimated to stand at 2,600.

The origins of Laxton are unclear, although evidence of a Roman villa has been found to the west of the village. The area had been settled by Saxon times and is referred to as Laxintune in the Domesday Book. It was also known as Lexington and by the thirteenth century the de Lexington family owned a substantial house within the village.

In the late eleventh and early twelfth century a motte and bailey type castle was constructed on the northern side of the village making Laxton an important place in medieval times. Royal visitors included Henry II and Edward I. Strategically situated on the eastern edge of Sherwood Forest, the castle had a defensive role and was also the venue for many forest courts. It fell into disuse in the fourteenth century.

During the sixteenth century a manor house was built to the southern side of the old castle site by the then lords of the manor, the Roos family. In 1621 this family sold the Manor of Laxton and the associated house was demolished later that century. Eventually the village passed into the hands of Earl Manvers whose family home was Thorseby Hall.

Laxton is famous for continuing the open field system of farming. Originating in the medieval period, most places stopped using the system when enclosure took place in the eighteenth century. It involved communities having two or three large fields with individuals working a number of narrow strips in each one. These fields were planted in a rotation of winter-sown wheat and spring-sown crops, before being allowed to lie fallow.

Although parts of Laxton have since been enclosed, the three main open fields, South Field, West Field and Mill Field, remain. Each year jurors are appointed to supervise the farming system and report to the court leet. Like most rural villages, much of the male population was once employed in agriculture. Laxton's population declined as the nineteenth century progressed, dropping from 642 in 1841 to 398 by 1911. The figure in 1981 stood at 294.

Today Laxton is famous not only as the last village operating the open field system, but also as the home of Beth Shalom, the National Holocaust Memorial Centre.

Windmills were an important feature in many agricultural areas in the nineteenth century, a period when Tuxford could boast two on Mill Mount. A post mill, dismantled *c*.1855, was replaced in 1874 by another mill of the same type which operated until about 1926. Close by was a four-storey tower mill built *c*.1820. This suffered extensive damage when it was struck by lightening in 1885, but was restored almost a century later between 1982 and 1993. Both mills can be made out in the background of this picture. Eldon Street looks very quiet, but the increased frequency and weight of traffic as the twentieth century progressed made it inevitable that the Great North Road would eventually be diverted around Tuxford.

The shop on Eldon Street beyond the Reindeer Inn (right foreground, with the lettering on the gable) was where Henry Norman Watson ran Tuxford post office between 1901 and 1921. He received the grand salary of £40. 19*s*. per annum. Letters arrived from Newark at 7.20 a.m. and 5 p.m. and were dispatched at 11.45 a.m. and 5.20. p.m. To supplement his income Mr Watson was also a newsagent and motor and cycle agent.

Tuxford's weekly market took place on a Monday. The market hall was built by the lord of the manor, the Duke of Newcastle, in 1852, and featured several arches in its main elevation, barred by iron gates to prevent unauthorised access. Known as the Butter Market, it was also the venue for the sale of eggs, poultry and fruit. By 1865 the weekly market was considered to be of 'little consequence' (*White's Directory*) and many buyers and sellers travelled to the flourishing sales at Newark or Retford instead. With the decline of Tuxford's market the building stood empty for many years until the decision was taken to demolish it in 1929. For a number of years prior to that the altar that now stands in St Mary Magdalene Chapel had been stored there.

The site made vacant after the knocking down of the market hall was acquired by Mr C. Talbot. He built commercial premises, seen here occupied by the Excelda Cafe. Passengers are boarding a single-decker bus for the journey to Newark, just over twelve miles away.

Comparisons between this picture and the one on page one show a number of changes. The cafe has a new sign and adverts in the window to the right. It is also operating as a branch of the National Provincial Bank. The building to the left has lost a window and gained a door. More significantly, the size of the market place has been reduced by the installation of a traffic island in the centre of it.

Newcastle Street was once known as Egmanton Street. The ivy-clad, bay-windowed house has today lost much of its grandeur, stripped of its greenery and with the wall and railings removed. It is called Newbridge House.

Newcastle Street was the site of the town lock-up, built in 1823 as its prominently displayed date stone tells us. The red-brick building, hidden behind the tree, had two cells where local miscreants were held until they could be dealt with by magistrates.

As well as a weekly market Tuxford also boasted two annual fairs: a livestock fair took place on 12 May until the outbreak of the First World War, and the hop fair was on 25 September but had ceased by 1865, as by then few hops were being grown locally. Apart from the little cottage second from the left, all these buildings on the left-hand side of Newcastle Street remain today.

Newcastle Street was where a devastating fire began on 8 September 1701. Because the houses were so close together, and much of what they were built with was flammable, the fire quickly took hold and caused extensive damage, destroying over 120 homes. Queen Anne and the Archbishop of York organised a nationwide appeal for alms to help the many destitute citizens of Tuxford.

Although the co-operative society shop remains at this site in Newcastle Street today, it has lost the characterful frontage seen here. The shop building next door with the polish and starch adverts is still standing, but the rest of the row as far as the car has been demolished.

The Sun Inn, left foreground, is situated at the corner of Newcastle Street. The importance of Tuxford as a post town is demonstrated by a warrant issued in 1638 which commanded thirty surrounding villages to be ready to supply the postmaster in Tuxford with post horses for the king's service when required.

Looking from the market hall towards Newark Road. During the town's annual May livestock fair the animals were carefully segregated. Horses were sold on Newcastle Street whilst cattle were kept here on Newark Road and sheep penned beyond the grammar school on Lincoln Road. This is a much earlier picture than the one on the previous page, with no sign of the three petrol pumps seen outside the three-storey building.

The grammar school, seen to the left flanking a badly surfaced Lincoln Road, was founded by Charles Read of Darlton in 1669. He had acquired his wealth from shipping and endowed the school with the rents from lands at Folkingham, Lincolnshire. The money helped to pay £20 annually for a master, and grants of £5 each to four worthy scholars.

Over the grammar school door is the motto 'What God Hath Built Let No Man Destroy'. The building closed as a school during the First World War, later seeing use as a children's clinic and an annex to Tuxford Primary School. It commenced its present use as the home of the local branch library in 1959.

By the beginning of the nineteenth century the principal inn in Tuxford was the Red Lion. This had been built on the site of the Crown, a traditional timber-framed, thatched-roofed building which survived a tremendous storm in 1587 but succumbed to the great fire of 1701. In 1828, following the arrival of a new lord of the manor, it became known as the Newcastle Arms Inn and Posting House.

The area in front of the Newcastle Arms Hotel was often used as a gathering point for the local hunt. The assembly rooms within the hotel were frequently the venue for hunt balls.

The precise date of establishment of Tuxford Parish Church is unclear, although a chapel of ease existed as early as 1179 and most of the building dates from the thirteenth to fifteenth centuries. A number of restoration projects have been carried out during its existence. In 1865 a new clock was fitted, and fourteen years later the spire had to be repaired after it was struck by lightning. In 1893 the sum of £1,500 was spent putting a new roof on the chancel and re-seating and re-flooring the church.

Looking into the market square with the church wall and railings to the right. The white building on the left with the steps up to its entrance was a local bank. Two cars are parked outside the Newcastle Arms, something that would be impossible today due to the congestion they would cause.

The eighteenth century vicarage stands opposite the church and is now in private ownership. In 1934 its replacement received a blessing from the Bishop of Southwell. For many years a quaint tradition took place at the vicarage each Maundy Thursday when dole loaves, made in the town bakery, were distributed.

The Tuxford Sunday school treat of 1912 featured the town band, as seen here.

In 1853, at the height of the travel boom on the Great North Road, Tuxford boasted eleven inns. There were five on Eldon Street (illustrated here), two each on Lincoln Street and Newcastle Street, and one on Mill Hill and London Road.

Eldon Street seen from the junction of the Ollerton road in the 1930s or 40s. The prominent sign on the right advertises Hewitt's Grimsby Ales. Earlier views (and trade directories) show the shop below the sign as being occupied by Edwin Smith, bootmaker and beer retailer, although the premises seem to have changed hands by the time this postcard was produced. The photographer has managed to capture a traffic-free scene, though a flock of sheep is strung out across the road in the distance.

The road leading from Tuxford towards Markham Moor, where motorists now have the choice of joining the A1 or continuing to the market town of Retford. Latterly the cottage to the left suffered major damage when it was hit by a lorry and as a result had to be demolished.

Looking up Eldon Street into Tuxford. The road surface had certainly improved since the early years of the twentieth century, reflecting the increase in the number of motor vehicles using it.

When the decision was taken to divert the A1 away from Tuxford the road was routed north of the town, close to the Markham Moor Inn.

On 31 December 1897 the Duchess of Newcastle paid a visit to Tuxford. As part of the celebrations to mark Queen Victoria's Diamond Jubilee she started the new quarter chimes on the church clock, after which she joined a procession from the church to the market place, led by Markham Brass Band, where she unveiled a new ornate street lamp.

On the listings detailing the 1799 Enclosure Award Lincoln Road has the less than pleasant name of Sludge Gate.

An interesting development took place on Lincoln Road (later renamed Lincoln Street) in 1800 when Sir Thomas White built Holywell Baths on the site of a natural mineral spring there. It was claimed that the waters provided a cure for rheumatism and scurvy, but reports stated that the baths attracted 'rowdy' elements on Sundays and consequently the baths were demolished in 1820.

In the early years of the twentieth century Lincoln Street was less built-up than today. During the Second World War a Land Army hostel was situated in this area of Tuxford. The town also housed evacuees from industrial districts that were being bombed, and troops were billeted in the area too.

Dukeries Junction station, opened by the Lancashire, Derbyshire & East Coast Railway Company, was to be found at Ashvale. Tuxford had four stations, with Tuxford North, Tuxford Central and Dukeries station being the other three. Large railway sheds were situated on the edge of the town employing much of the adult male population.

For many years the White family lived in the manor house close to the church, but in 1698 the main family home became Wallingwalls in the north of the county. Tuxford Hall was constructed on the site of a previous mansion in 1785.

One former owner of Tuxford Hall, Robert Stratton Wilson, fell out with the vicar when he wasn't made church warden and in a fit of pique built a large meeting room on the side of the hall in which to hold rival services.

Robert Stratton Wilson was something of an eccentric and excavated a wide hole in the grounds of the hall which he termed 'The Hell'. Into this he would place models of people and 'demons' that had displeased him. He added notes of complaint to characters such as King Alcohol, the Tobacco Devil, Superstition, Priestcraft, the Religious Lawyer and the Woman with the Proud Look and the Lying Tongue. After his death the models were sold and 'The Hell' dismantled.

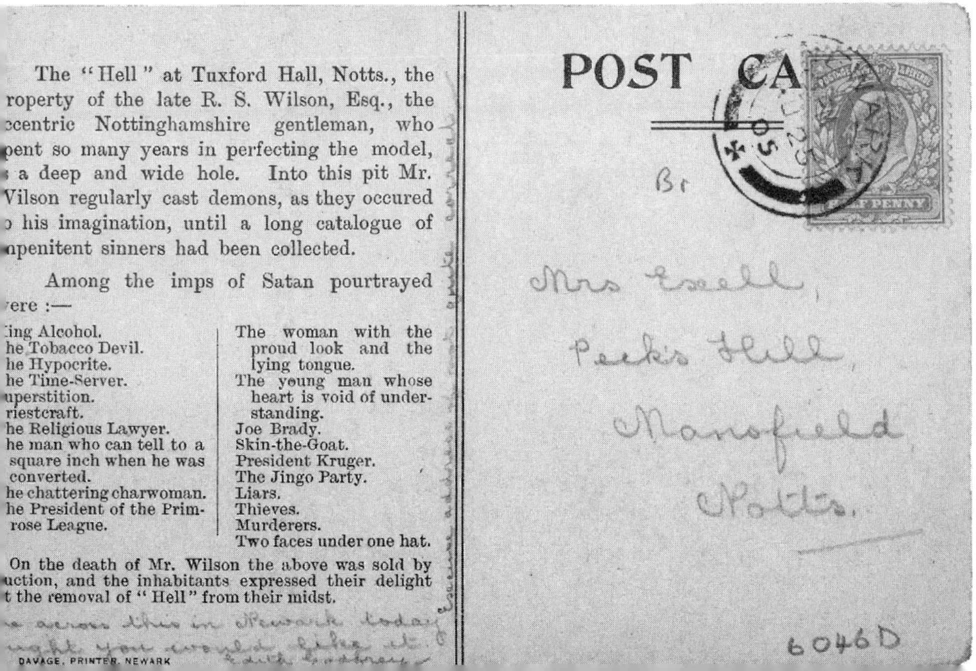

The "Hell" at Tuxford Hall, Notts., the roperty of the late R. S. Wilson, Esq., the ccentric Nottinghamshire gentleman, who pent so many years in perfecting the model, a deep and wide hole. Into this pit Mr. Vilson regularly cast demons, as they occured o his imagination, until a long catalogue of npenitent sinners had been collected.

Among the imps of Satan pourtrayed vere :—

ing Alcohol.
he Tobacco Devil.
he Hypocrite.
he Time-Server.
uperstition.
riestcraft.
he Religious Lawyer.
he man who can tell to a square inch when he was converted.
he chattering charwoman.
he President of the Primrose League.
The woman with the proud look and the lying tongue.
The young man whose heart is void of understanding.
Joe Brady.
Skin-the-Goat.
President Kruger.
The Jingo Party.
Liars.
Thieves.
Murderers.
Two faces under one hat.

On the death of Mr. Wilson the above was sold by uction, and the inhabitants expressed their delight t the removal of "Hell" from their midst.

DAVAGE, PRINTER, NEWARK

POST CA

Mrs Esell,
Peck's Hill,
Mansfield,
Notts.

6046D

The presence of the castle helped to make Laxton a prosperous place, and the village's church reflected this wealth. It dates from 1190 with thirteenth century extensions. Within the church are thirteenth and fourteenth century monuments to the de Everingham family. Over the years, as the importance of Laxton declined, so did its church. A significant remodelling took place in 1860 when it was reduced in size and parts of it were rebuilt.

Laxton vicarage was built in 1875 by John Birch and cost £2,769. Its first occupant was the Revd Henry Arthur Martin, vicar of the parish from 1858 to 1898. Today, like many Victorian vicarages, it no longer belongs to the church.

The tower of St Michael's Church, which houses six bells, seems to dominate everything in Laxton. It was rebuilt with stone from the original tower during the renovations of 1860, the cap of the new structure being an innovation at the time. The cottages with skylights in their roofs separate the entrance to the church grounds from the drive to the rectory.

Egmanton Road leading into Laxton. At the bottom of the hill the road divides, with Cross Hill branching to the right and the road to Moorhouse to the left.

The Dovecote Inn began life as a farmhouse and is first recorded as a pub in 1832. By the 1840s four inns operated in Laxton, but at the end of the nineteenth century only the Dovecote remained. It is still the venue for the annual court leet which presides over the ancient open field system.

Pupils of Laxton School have gathered across the roadway outside the school (on the right and now the village hall) for a photograph. Earl Manvers met the cost of £483 when the building was erected in 1860. The school closed in 1947.

These children were photographed outside Church Farm in 1912. At this time the infant department was segregated from the main village school, and the younger children received their education in premises on this side of the road.

The village shop and post office remains in this building today, although the advertising signs have been removed.

The house to the left with the windows in its gable has now gone, and a new building called Smithy Farm, dated 1966, has been erected on this section of road. The barns to the right stand next to Ivy House Farm.

This postcard, looking into Laxton from the Ollerton Road, was sent in 1912. Horse-drawn carts, such as the one pulled up across the road in the middle distance, were a common form of transport in rural and urban areas at this time.

At the far end of the village the road divides. To the left it carries traffic towards Boughton and Ollerton, while to the right is Town End, providing access to West Field. The cottages in the V of the junction have since been demolished. Home View Farm, with a pig and a sheep rooting around peacefully in front of it, remains today, as does the house beyond it.

The photographer was standing with his back to the entrance to West Field, one of the three areas of the open field system, when he took this view. The car is parked outside Town End Farm. Top Farm was further down the road on the right. During enemy bombing on 28 August 1940 a bomb landed in West Field, exploding and leaving a large crater. More seriously, many windows were shattered in the village and one resident, Miss Barbara Willis, was killed outside the door of the schoolhouse.

The haystack with the ladder leaning against it is outside Twitchell Farmhouse. The tree in the centre of the picture can still be identified today.

Here a car is parked by the side of an outbuilding belonging to Twitchell Cottage. In the early years of the twentieth century this was the site of the village post office.

These brick cottages with York tiled roofs and incongruous mock-Tudor gable ends formed part of the Laxton Estate. The Manvers family sold the estate to the Ministry of Agriculture in 1952, and during the latter's period of ownership parts of it were disposed of, including some of these cottages.

Where the open field system of farming operated, farmsteads such as this one were often in the centre of the village rather than scattered around the edge of the community. Many properties were constructed with their gable ends to the road allowing more buildings to have access to the village streets.